Cambridge Discovery Readers

Starter Level

Series editor: Nicholas Tims

Gone!

Margaret Johnson

CAMBRIDGE
UNIVERSITY PRESS

University Printing House, Cambridge CB2 8BS, United Kingdom

One Liberty Plaza, 20th Floor, New York, NY 10006, USA

477 Williamstown Road, Port Melbourne, VIC 3207, Australia

314–321, 3rd Floor, Plot 3, Splendor Forum, Jasola District Centre,
New Delhi – 110025, India

79 Anson Road, #06–04/06, Singapore 079906

Cambridge University Press is part of the University of Cambridge.

It furthers the University's mission by disseminating knowledge in the pursuit of
education, learning and research at the highest international levels of excellence.

www.cambridge.org

This American English edition is based on *Gone!*, ISBN 978-8-483-23509-6
first published by Cambridge University Press in 2009.

First published 2009
American English edition 2010

20 19 18 17 16 15 14 13 12 11 10 9 8 7 6

Printed in Great Britain by CPI Group (UK) Ltd, Croydon CR0 4YY

ISBN 978-0-521-14904-4 Paperback American English edition

No character in this work is based on any person living or dead.
Any resemblance to an actual person or situation is purely accidental.

Illustrations by Lyn Knott

Audio recording by hyphen

Exercises by Peter McDonnell

The publishers are grateful to the following for permission to reproduce
photographic material:

Getty Images | Timothy Allen for cover image

Contents

People in the story

Jamie: a boy with a birthday
Mom: Jamie's mother
Angie: Jamie's sister
Dad: Jamie's father
Blake: Jamie's friend

BEFORE YOU READ

1 Look at the pictures in Chapter 1. What do you think?
   Answer the questions.

   1 How old is Jamie?

   ....

   2 Does Jamie have a big sister?

   ....

   3 Does Jamie's mother work?

   ....

Chapter 1

Birthday boy

"I'm sorry I'm working on your birthday, Jamie."

Jamie's mother is leaving the house. She isn't looking at Jamie. She's thinking about work.

"Have a nice day, honey. See you tonight," she says.

"Good-bye, Mom," Jamie says. He feels sad. He doesn't want her to go.

Jamie's sister, Angie, comes down from her room. "Happy birthday, little brother!" she says. "Twelve today!"

Jamie smiles. He likes being twelve.

"Can I give you your birthday present[1] this afternoon?" Angie asks. "I'm going to the mall with my friends this morning." She goes to the door.

"I want to go to the mall," Jamie starts to say, but Angie doesn't hear.

"Enjoy your birthday," she says. Then she leaves, too.

Now Jamie's father is the only person at home[2]. Jamie finds him at his desk. He's working on his computer. Jamie's father works at home, and he works all the time. Jamie walks into his father's office and his father turns and looks at him. "Hi, Jamie," he says. "What are you going to do with your birthday money?"

"I don't know, Dad," Jamie says. "Can we go to the mall?"

Jamie's father is looking at his computer again. "Not today, Jamie," he says. "I have to finish this work. Where's Angie?"

"She's at the mall with her friends," Jamie says.

He knows his father isn't listening. He's reading an e-mail on his computer.

"That's nice," he says, but he doesn't look at Jamie. "Have a good time!"

"OK," says Jamie and he leaves the room.

Jamie calls his friend Blake. Blake's mother answers.

"Can I speak to Blake?" Jamie asks.

"I'm sorry," Blake's mother says. "He's playing soccer in Winston Park³. Is this Jamie?"

"Yes," says Jamie.

"Blake tells me it's your birthday today," Blake's mother says. "Happy birthday!"

"Thank you," says Jamie.

"I have to go, but have a good day!" says Blake's mother.

"Thank you," Jamie says again and he puts the phone down.

"No one has any time for me today," he thinks. "It's my birthday and no one has any time for me."

LOOKING BACK

1 Check your answers to *Before you read* on page 4.

ACTIVITIES

2 Complete the sentences with the names in the box.

Jamie (x3)   Mom   Dad   Angie (x2)   Blake (x2)

1 ....*Mom*.... leaves the house and goes to work.
2 .... is Jamie's sister.
3 It's ....'s birthday.
4 .... is twelve today.
5 .... is going to the mall.
6 .... works at home.
7 .... is Jamie's friend.
8 .... is at the park.
9 .... isn't happy.

3 Underline the correct words in each sentence.
1 Mom is thinking about *her work* / *Jamie's birthday*.
2 Angie *has* / *doesn't have* a present for Jamie.
3 Jamie's *father* / *mother* has a computer.
4 Jamie *has some* / *doesn't have any* birthday money.
5 Jamie's father *can* / *can't* go to the mall.
6 Dad is *listening to Jamie* / *reading his e-mail*.
7 Jamie speaks to *Blake* / *Blake's mother*.
8 Blake *knows* / *doesn't know* it's Jamie's birthday.

4 Who do the <u>underlined</u> words refer to in these lines from the text?

> Angie (x2)   Jamie   Dad
>
> Mom   Jamie and Dad   Blake

1 "See <u>you</u> tonight." (page 5) ....*Jamie*........

2 He doesn't want <u>her</u> to go. (page 6) ....

3 <u>She</u> goes to the door. (page 7) ....

4 Jamie finds <u>him</u> at his desk. (page 7) ....

5 "Can <u>we</u> go to the mall?" (page 8) ....

6 "She's at the mall with <u>her</u> friends." (page 8) ....

7 "<u>He</u>'s playing soccer in Winston Park." (page 9) ....

5 Match the questions with the answers.

1 Why is today a special day for Jamie? ☐ *6*

2 What does Jamie get for his birthday? ☐

3 What does Jamie's dad do at home? ☐

4 Who does Jamie talk to on the phone? ☐

5 Who is playing soccer? ☐

a He works.

b̶ It's his birthday.

c Blake's mother.

d He gets some money.

e Blake.

LOOKING FORWARD

6 Check (✓) what you think happens in Chapter 2.

1 Jamie goes to the park. ☐

2 Jamie stays at home. ☐

The camera

Jamie leaves the house and walks to Winston Park. He doesn't like soccer, but he wants to be with people.

It's a hot day. In Winston Park there are lots of mothers and fathers with their children. Boys and girls are running and laughing. Everyone looks happy. Jamie sees Blake and some more boys. They're playing soccer.

Jamie goes over. Blake sees him. He smiles. "Hi, Jamie!" he calls. "Happy birthday!"

"Thank you!" Jamie calls, but Blake is running to get the ball.

Jamie watches the game[4] for ten minutes, but Blake doesn't speak to him again. Blake's good at soccer and he's enjoying the game. Jamie starts walking across Winston Park.

He sits down on a seat and takes a drink from his bag.

He puts his bag down. There is another bag under the seat.

"What's this?" thinks Jamie. The bag is black. Jamie opens it. He's looking for a name. There is only one thing in the bag: a camera.

Jamie takes it out. Then he looks in the bag again, but there is nothing in it. No name.

Jamie looks at the camera. There are four buttons: PHOTO, DELETE, ON, and OFF.

Jamie puts his finger on the ON button and presses[5] it. The camera makes a noise.

The black bag is on the seat. Jamie can see it in the camera. Jamie puts his finger on the PHOTO button. He presses it. The camera makes another noise. Jamie looks at the picture of the bag. It's OK, but he doesn't want a picture of a bag, so he presses the DELETE button. The picture goes away.

"This camera is OK," Jamie thinks. "But it isn't my camera. I have to take it to the police. I can buy a camera with my birthday money."

Jamie puts out his hand to take the camera bag from the seat. But the bag isn't there.

He looks under the seat. No bag. He looks behind the seat. No bag. Jamie doesn't understand. "Where is the bag?" he thinks.

A squirrel runs in front of the seat. Jamie wants a picture of it. The squirrel stops.

"It's looking for food," Jamie thinks. He smiles and presses the PHOTO button. But when he looks at the picture, it isn't good.

"Squirrels are too fast for pictures," Jamie thinks.

He presses the DELETE button. The picture of the squirrel goes away.

When Jamie looks for the squirrel, he can't see it.

"Squirrels run fast," Jamie thinks. "But not that fast. Where is it?"

Jamie looks at the camera. He doesn't understand. Something is wrong. He wants to try the camera again. There are some flowers next to his seat. Jamie looks at the camera again. He can see the flowers. He presses the PHOTO button and takes a picture of the flowers.

Then he presses the DELETE button to make the picture go away. Jamie takes the camera away from his face. He looks for the flowers. They aren't there.

"The flowers are gone," he thinks. "Gone!"

LOOKING BACK

1 Check your answer to *Looking forward* on page 11.

ACTIVITIES

2 <u>Underline</u> the correct words in each sentence.

1 Jamie <u>*wants*</u> / *doesn't want* to be with friends.
2 Jamie *plays soccer with* / *talks to* Blake.
3 Blake *is* / *isn't* good at soccer.
4 Jamie has something to *eat* / *drink* in the park.
5 *Jamie* / *Blake* finds a camera.
6 Jamie *uses* / *doesn't use* the camera.
7 Jamie wants to take the camera *to the police* / *home*.
8 Jamie deletes *all* / *some of* his pictures.

3 Put the sentences in order.

1 Jamie finds a camera. ☐
2 Jamie speaks to Blake. ☐
3 Jamie sits down. ☐
4 Jamie goes to the park. ☐
5 Jamie deletes the picture. ☐
6 Jamie watches the game. ☐
7 Jamie takes a picture of the bag. ☐
8 The bag is gone. ☐

4 Are the sentences true (*T*) or false (*F*)?

1 Jamie runs to the park. ☐F

2 The weather is good. ☐

3 Jamie doesn't watch all the game. ☐

4 Jamie finds a blue bag under his seat. ☐

5 There's nothing in the bag. ☐

6 The camera has three buttons. ☐

7 Jamie takes a picture of his bag. ☐

8 Jamie doesn't like his picture of the squirrel. ☐

5 Answer the questions.

1 Does Jamie like soccer?

....

2 Where does Jamie find the bag?

....

3 What does he look for in the bag?

....

4 Is the picture of the squirrel good? Why / Why not?

....

LOOKING FORWARD

6 Check (✓) what you think happens in the next two chapters.

1 Jamie plays soccer. ☐

2 Jamie takes more pictures with the camera. ☐

3 Jamie goes to the mall. ☐

Chapter 3

Where's the ball?

Jamie puts the camera down. He doesn't want it in his hands now. He feels afraid[6].

He thinks about the camera bag, the squirrel, and the flowers.

"When I take pictures of things with this camera, they go away," he thinks. "I don't know how, but they do."

Across Winston Park he can see the boys playing soccer.

"I have to tell Blake about this!" he thinks. He puts the camera in his bag and starts running across the park.

But after a minute he stops running. He thinks about the camera bag, the squirrel, and the flowers again. He's near the boys now.

"It's my birthday," he thinks. "I want Blake to come to the mall with me. We can get a pizza. I can buy something with my birthday money."

A boy in a blue T-shirt has the ball now. He's running fast. Then everyone shouts.

"Goal!"

Lots of the boys run to the boy in the blue T-shirt. They are all very happy.

Jamie quickly takes the camera from the bag and looks into it. He can see the ball.

He presses the PHOTO button and then the DELETE button. The boys want to start playing again.

"Hey!" shouts the boy in the blue T-shirt. "Where's the ball?"

No one can understand. They look on the grass[7] and behind trees.

"Can you see the ball, Jamie?" Blake asks.

"No, sorry," Jamie says. "I don't know where the ball is. I don't think you can play now. Do you want to get a pizza with me? I can buy something to eat with my birthday money."

But Blake doesn't hear Jamie. He's listening to the boy in the blue T-shirt.

"It's OK," he says. "I have another ball in my bag."

"Good," says Blake. "But where is our other ball?"

"I don't know," says the boy.

He gets the new ball from his bag. They start to play again.

Jamie thinks about taking a new picture: a picture of the new ball. But the boys run away across the grass, and Jamie turns and starts to walk home.

Chapter 4

The computer

When Jamie gets home, his father is making coffee.

"Jamie? Is that you?" he calls.

"Yes," Jamie answers.

"Do you want coffee?" his father asks.

"No thank you," answers Jamie. "I'm just getting something from my room."

Jamie quickly runs up to his father's office. It's the room with the computer. He takes the camera from his bag. He can see the computer in it. He quickly presses PHOTO. Then DELETE.

He looks at the table. No computer.

"Good," he thinks.

Jamie's father comes into the room with his coffee. He smiles at Jamie.

"Are you OK?" he asks. Then he stops smiling. "Where's my computer?" he asks.

"I don't know," says Jamie.

"I don't understand," Jamie's father says. "Where is it?" He looks behind Jamie. He looks under the table. He looks all over the room. Then he looks at Jamie.

"Jamie?" he says. "Where's my computer?"

"I don't know," answers Jamie.

"Computers don't just go away!" Jamie's father says.

"Yes they do!" thinks Jamie.

Then he looks at his father. "Can we go to the mall, Dad?" he asks.

"No, Jamie!" his father says. "I have to find my computer! I'm going to call the police."

"After the police come," Jamie says, "can we go to the mall then?"

But Jamie's father can't stop thinking about his computer.

"Please, Jamie," he says. He looks tired. "I know it's your birthday, but all my work is on that computer. It's very important. I don't know what to do."

Jamie looks at his father.

"I'm sorry, Dad," he says.

His father smiles a little. "It's OK, son," he says. "Go and enjoy your birthday."

Jamie leaves the room. "I can't enjoy my birthday," he thinks. "No one has any time for me."

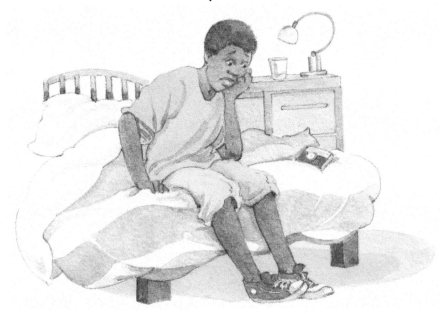

Jamie goes to his room and sits on his bed. Then he thinks about his mother and he knows what he wants to do.

LOOKING BACK

1 Check your answer to *Looking forward* on page 23.

ACTIVITIES

2 <u>Underline</u> the correct words in each sentence.
1 Jamie *tells / <u>doesn't tell</u>* his friend about the camera.
2 Jamie wants to *eat something / play soccer* with Blake.
3 Jamie takes a picture of the *ball / boy*.
4 The boys continue playing with *a new / the old* ball.
5 Jamie *takes / doesn't take* a picture of the new ball.
6 Jamie's dad is *working / making a drink* when Jamie gets home.
7 When Jamie gets home, he goes to his *bedroom / dad's office*.
8 Jamie's dad's computer is important because it has a lot of *work / pictures* on it.
9 Jamie *is / isn't* enjoying his birthday.

3 Answer the questions.
In Chapters 3 and 4, who ...
1 is afraid? *Jamie*
2 asks Jamie about the ball? ....
3 finds another ball in his bag? ....
4 makes a drink? ....
5 loses his computer? ....
6 can't do any work? ....
7 wants to go to the mall? ....
8 isn't happy? ....

4 Match the two parts of the sentences.

1 Jamie runs across the park because [c]
2 Jamie doesn't take a picture of the new ball because ☐
3 Jamie's dad isn't in his office because ☐
4 Jamie wants the computer to go away because ☐
5 Jamie can't enjoy his birthday because ☐

a he's making coffee.
b no one has any time for him.
c he wants to tell Blake about the camera.
d he wants to go to the mall with his dad.
e the boys run away.

5 Answer the questions.

1 Why does Jamie put the camera down at the start of Chapter 3?

....

2 What does Jamie want to do with his birthday money?

....

3 How many pictures does Jamie take in Chapters 3 and 4?

....

LOOKING FORWARD

6 Check (✓) what you think happens in the final chapter.

1 Jamie goes to see his mom at work. ☐
2 He takes the camera to the police. ☐
3 He buys a new camera. ☐

Chapter 5

Trying to help

Jamie leaves the house and walks to his mother's café – Kathy's Coffee Shop.

The café sells food all day. Lots of people go there on Saturdays. Jamie can see his mother in the café. She looks hot. There are people at all the tables and they're all waiting for their food.

"Mom's tired," Jamie thinks. "She works a lot."

He goes into the café.

His mother sees him.

"Hi, Jamie," she says. "Why are you here on your birthday?"

"I'm here to help you," he says.

His mother smiles.

"Oh, thank you, Jamie," she says. "People want plates and cups for their food and drinks," she says. "They're all dirty."

She takes Jamie to the dirty plates and cups in the kitchen[8].

"Can you wash them for me?" she asks.

Jamie smiles.

"Of course," he says.

Jamie's mother smiles again.

"You're a good boy," she says. Then she leaves the kitchen.

Jamie quickly takes the camera from his bag.

"I can have an afternoon with Mom," he thinks. "We can go to a restaurant. Or watch a movie."

He can see the dirty cups and plates in the camera. He presses PHOTO. Then DELETE. Then he takes the camera away and looks.

"Gone," he thinks. "They're gone." And he smiles.

His mother comes back into the kitchen. She looks all over the room.

"Jamie?" she says. "Where are the cups and plates?"

Jamie thinks for a few[9] seconds.

"It's the camera," he tells her. "When I take a picture, things go away."

His mother looks at him. She looks very tired now. "What?" she asks. "I don't understand."

"The camera …" Jamie starts, but his mother speaks.

"Jamie," she says, "there aren't any plates or cups and there are lots of people in the café. What am I going to do?"

"Close the café, Mom," Jamie says. "We can go out."

His mother is angry now.

"I can't close the café, Jamie!" she says. "This is my job! Now, please, tell me where the cups and plates are."

"I don't know, Mom," Jamie starts saying. "It's the camera …"

The door opens. Jamie's sister comes in.

"Hi," she says. "What's wrong?"

Jamie's mother starts telling Angie about the plates and cups, but Angie isn't listening. She sees Jamie's camera.

"What's this?" she says and takes it from her brother. "Is it new?"

"Give it to me!" Jamie says.

Angie doesn't listen. She puts the camera to her eye. She looks at Jamie.

"Smile!" she says.

"No!" Jamie shouts.
Angie presses the PHOTO button.
"Give the camera to me, Angie!" Jamie shouts.
Angie looks at the picture.

"This isn't a good picture of you, Jamie," Angie says.
"No! Don't press any buttons!" shouts Jamie.
But it's too late. Angie presses DELETE.

LOOKING BACK

1 Check your answer to *Looking forward* on page 37.

ACTIVITIES

2 Put the sentences in order.
1 Jamie and his mom go into the kitchen. ☐
2 Angie takes the camera from Jamie. ☐
3 Jamie takes a picture of the cups and plates. ☐
4 Angie takes a picture of Jamie. ☐
5 Jamie goes to his mom's work. ☐ *1*
6 Jamie tells his mom about the camera. ☐
7 Angie arrives at the café. ☐
8 The cups and plates go away. ☐

3 Match the two parts of the sentences.
1 Jamie goes to the café because ☐ *d*
2 Jamie takes a picture of the cups and plates because ☐
3 Jamie's mom wants the cups and plates because ☐
4 Jamie's mom is angry because ☐
5 Angie presses DELETE because ☐

a the cups and plates are gone.
b it isn't a good picture of Jamie.
c there are lots of people in the café.
d he wants to go out with his mom.
e he doesn't want to wash them.

46

4 Are the sentences true (*T*) or false (*F*)?

1 It's the weekend. ☐ *T*
2 Jamie's mom has a lot of work at the café. ☐
3 She's happy because Jamie wants to help her. ☐
4 Jamie doesn't want to wash the cups and plates. ☐
5 Jamie tells his mom about the camera. ☐
6 Jamie's mom can't close the café. ☐
7 Jamie tells Angie about the camera. ☐
8 Angie takes a picture of Jamie with her camera. ☐

5 Underline the correct words in each sentence.

1 *There are a lot of* / *There aren't any* people in Kathy's Coffee Shop.
2 *Jamie* / *Jamie's mom* is tired.
3 The cups and plates are *on the tables* / *in the kitchen*.
4 *Jamie* / *Jamie's mom* tells Angie about the cups and plates.
5 Angie *listens* / *doesn't listen* to Jamie.

6 Answer the questions.

1 Why is Jamie's mom surprised to see him in the café?

....

2 What is Jamie's plan?

....

3 What happens when Angie takes a picture of Jamie?

....

4 List the things that are "gone" in the story.

....

Glossary

[1]**present** (page 7) *noun*　something that you give to someone, often on a special day, for example birthdays

[2]**home** (page 7) *noun*　the place where you live

[3]**park** (page 9) *noun*　a big area of **grass**, often in a town, where people can walk and play

[4]**game** (page 14) *noun*　an activity or sport that people play

[5]**press** (page 16) *verb*　to push something hard

[6]**afraid** (page 24) *adjective*　scared or worried

[7]**grass** (page 28) *noun*　a green plant that grows on the ground in gardens and **parks**

[8]**kitchen** (page 40) *noun*　a room that you cook food in

[9]**(a) few** (page 42)　some, or a small number of